Never Alone
in a
Cemetery

Rick Taylor

Copyright © 2017 by Rick Taylor

All rights reserved. No part of this book may be reproduced in any form or by any electronic or mechanical means including photocopying, recording and information storage and retrieval systems—except in the case of brief quotations imbedded in critical articles or reviews—without the permission in writing from the author.

Cover & Book Design: Scribe Freelance
www.scribefreelance.com

Published by:

CEZNO PRESS

ISBN: 978-1-933704-99-9

Printed in the United States of America

Contents

Never Alone in a Cemetery 7
Forever Frick 8
Section 12 9
Plumed Harbinger 10
Red-Tail 11
Last Supper 12
The Big Snow 13
Wind Chimes 14
Encampment 15
Silent Sentinels 16
Lynching 17
Hard Wind 18
Mole in a Hole 19
Pretty Rich Girl 20
A Pixie from Texas 22
Uncle Charlie 23
Along the Lake 24
Suicide in Blawnox 25
Beating the Rain 26
Squaw Valley Park 27
Saturday Matinee 28
Rip-Off 29
New Perspectives 30
My Uncle is a Steering Knob 32
My Sister was a Warner Brothers Wannabe 33
Indian Display 34
I'm Here on my Deathbed 35
Butterfly 36

Dunmoyle 37
Elmira 39
D'Aleppo 40
Blood-Red 43
Left Behind 44
Becoming Part of Nature 46
Ode to Benjy 47
An Ancient Eye 49
Rally 50
South China Sea 51
Musings of a Death Camp Commandant 52
Lost Body Parts 53
Lawrence, Kansas 54
Hijinks During the Grand Review 56
Goya's Revenge 57
Winston Envy 58
Body Double 59
Upon Observing a Photograph of Hemingway in His Later Years 60
I'm James Dean 62
Hubris 63
Homage to Shelley at Seaside 64
Being Etta Place 65
A Key Lesson 67
Blitzkrieg 69
Ours Are Do-Nothing Days 70
Great Works Bring Everlasting Fame 71
As Time Goes By 72
Time Doesn't Leave Us Alone 73
Watch Out 74

Where Did It All Go?	76
Aged Fruit	77
Dust to Dust	78
Footprint	79
The Bullet Train	80
Time is Now No Friend to Me	81
Lucinda in Pursuit	82
The Big Bang	83
Swoosh	84
Lucinda in Peril	85
Blind	87
Foxfire	88
Harrier	89
Gilberte	90
Lucinda	92
Time to Walk the Ocean Floor	94
Dreams by Moonlight	95
Aquatic Creatures	96
A Coach and Four	97
Dreams	98
Pinch-Penny	99
Poolside with the President	100
Matadors at the Slaughterhouse	101
Water Hole	102
Do Horses Think of Suicide?	103
Coo	104
Ode to a Blue Jay	106
Beyond the Beasts	108
On Display	109

Alice's Lament	110
Publicity Blitz	111
Learning About Horses	112
Will Zu Zu Come Through?	113
Kong Wrong	114
Colossal Beans	116
Bugged	118
Big Things Have Feelings Too	120
A Pointless Exercise	121
Brain Suctioning Through a Tube	122
A Bad Rap	123
Three Troikas	124
Aristototelian Musings	125
Pricked	126
Misplaced Humor	127
The Human Body is a Miracle	128

Never Alone in a Cemetery

Never alone
in a cemetery,
I walk
down Millionaire's Row
whose members
are just as quiet,
dead silent,
as the common folk.
There are no dolmens,
menhirs or cromlechs here.
And the obelisks,
rare as they are,
do not compare
to the massive monoliths of old.
But the same starlings
our ancestors knew,
hundreds and hundreds of them,
still startle *en masse*
at some foreign sound
to pulverize the sky
before alighting once more,
dead black upon the ground
eternally.

Forever Frick

They're all here—
both Henrys, Adelaide, Helen,
even "Rose Bud,"
tiny Martha,
who swallowed the fatal pin—
all blanketed now in snow
and silent
as I pass
in winter's sunlight
on the same hill
that thirteen horses had to overcome
as they pulled the huge Frick cenotaph
into place.
Nearby, leafless oaks
encrusted with frozen rain
dangle their diamonds
before the sleeping family
in a vain attempt
to awaken them.

Section 12

You'll find them
in Homewood Cemetery,
boy soldiers
once clad in Union blue—
Emmett, Elroy, Daniel,
Joshua and the rest
many too young for a first love,
all with dreams unfulfilled
spread out in a valley
marked Section 12
beneath headstones
hardly noticeable
from the road above,
asleep in even rows
far from exploding shells,
shrieking horses,
cursing wounded,
rattling musketry,
blaring bugles
and pounding drums.
Instead, there is only peace
in this quiet place
as the rain offers tears
to wipe away
any inscriptions
tied to their memory.

Plumed Harbinger

O plumed harbinger!
you stand the graveyard shift,
a motionless silhouette against the moon,
a silent sentinel that presages our darkest endings.
When you appear in my own back yard
I'm terrified at first
until you ask *whooooo?*
which is a relief
since you can't have selected me
if you don't know my name.

Red-Tail

Circling the afternoon sun,
she presents an aureole
of gleaming feathers,
a translucent canopy,
before hurtling to earth
like some red-tailed meteor.

With catch secured,
she soars upward again
to her nest in a high evergreen,
a sacristy in the cemetery
offering one tiny head
to acknowledge
this noble deed.

The tenderness
that feeds this tiny mouth
belies the savagery
that enveloped the solitary rabbit
caught in a final scamper
among the headstones.
The bloodbath that follows
alerts the marble angel
who, leaning forward,
blesses the rite of sacrifice
with outstretched wings.

Last Supper

Cancer was just a word
ten years ago
when first we saw
your greenish eyes
leering at us through the film.

Ovarian and deadly
your tumor's shadow
becomes for us
a harbinger
portending its sure return.

At the Club last night
we find our seats
past lingering tables
of contented diners
until your talons set.

In departure along the parquet floor
we wonder if the occupants notice
the empty table
the uneaten food
and the slow walk toward the door.

The Big Snow

Deep snow.
Up to my thighs.
Rising moon.
Father and I trudge uphill
to the neighborhood toboggan run.
A nearby steel-barreled fire
punches yellow holes
in the darkness.
I think of Adrianne
who lives nearby.
And when she appears in silhouette,
I envision her full lips
and long, flowing hair.
My father knows nothing of my love for her
yet it is he who suggests to her brothers
that she and I go alone
on the very next run.
Adrianne ends up in my lap and in my arms
during an ecstatic rush
that carries my emotions to the very brink.
Later, when my mother asks my father
how the tobogganing went
he says nothing,
but gives her a knowing wink.

Wind Chimes

The tinkling sound of a wind chime
bores into my memory.
What better way to write about silence
than to highlight a sound like this?

Dana discovers the best approach right away
to the delight of our Professor,
who assures her right off that her story
highlighting tinkling chimes, melodious toads,
chirping crickets and one small owl—
is publishable at once.

Meanwhile, my own paper is little noted
nor long remembered.
Our Professor doesn't buy it.
Jumping past any reference to sounds at all,
I write, It was quiet, really quiet.

Encampment

My bath
warm and soothing,
brings back a memory
of my younger years,
after Mother granted my request
to let me stay home from school.
The same sense of release,
the same feeling of exultation
I'm feeling now
would come to me in those days
as I lay alone in bed
playing with my lead soldiers.
They responded to my every command
As they marched and fought
in the blanket folds.

But now the focus shifts
as I recall that it was Mother
who insisted that I give my soldiers away
to my Father's boss,
who desired them
for his son.
How quickly the water chills,
as I emerge
dripping from that memory.

Silent Sentinels

A high school pennant
above my daughter's bed
is recently joined by a second
touting the university
where she meets a student
who turns out to be
the man whom she will wed.

A lamb, a crocodile and a bear
now sit now alone on Lindsay's bed.
I ask them—
Why would she leave me?
She is too young to be involved
in a permanent vacation?
The three blank faces stare back at me
offering no explanation.

Lynching

Look there, Father says.
See what we do to Niggers.
A young man,
no older than my sister
dangles from a rope
slowly turning,
his black skin
blacker because of the burning.
Years later,
with my bigoted father safely dead,
I returned to that infamous spot.
Although the gnarled tree
was free of marks
the mind-corpse in my head
was still turning, refusing to rot.

Hard Wind

The beach at Lewes
gives access to a Sunfish,
tiny, single-masted,
the perfect craft to test my skill (such as it is).
Alone at the helm,
I provide a convincing show
until whitecaps become
the watery precursor
to a deadly blow.
Back over my shoulder
I spot one tiny figure
on the beach, watching me,
apparently concerned (and correctly so)
that I'll be blown out to sea.
Under my breath I pray
for success in turning the craft about.
It takes all the strength I have,
and with a thrust and an extended shout
I'm able to do it.
Back on the beach, exhausted and trembling.
I find it somewhat odd
that my willing protector
looks nothing at all like a god.
Instead, he is bald,
not tall, wearing disheveled clothing
and reeking of alcohol.

Mole in a Hole

A deep pit on a construction site
offers no escape for a tiny mole
as young boys
throw heavy clogs of dirt
into the gaping hole.
Stop before you kill
That innocent creature.
But the words are stuck in my throat.
Afraid to speak
or to block
the repeated attacks,
I simply wait
for the bloody climax
that eventually comes.
Back then
it's easy to rationalize.
After all,
I'm only ten
and the mole is very small.

Pretty Rich Girl

It was like drinking champagne
from a plastic cup
or wearing jeans to church.
My attraction to you was out of place.
You were a physician's daughter
from Fox Chapel
and I a poor boy from Highland Park.
I remember first seeing you
on your horse,
your auburn hair
ablaze in the morning sun.
Color-wise the mare
was your sister in beauty,
ready for her morning run
and you up top,
the pretty rich girl.
And, oh, how I loved you
from the moment
I first saw you
on that gallant horse of yours.
Ten times a day your image
would appear,
featuring emblazoned hair
that always set my heart afire.
Coward that I was,
and young,
I never called you,
never spoke to you.
The ultimate rejection,
although imagined

and just as painful,
came from me and not from you.

A Pixie from Texas

She has captured my heart
this Pixie from Texas
whose smile assures me
that we'll never be apart.
We are joined in a magnificent
pairing that from the start
offers proof of her generosity
intelligence and caring.

I'm blessed that she's elected
to marry me, a struggling
writer and poet whose light
has yet to shine.
Who can doubt
that her love and brilliance
will charge my engines,
reset my course
and turn my watery
poetry into wine?

Uncle Charlie

None of the grownups
ever thought Uncle Charlie
would amount to a hill of beans.
After all, he'd flunked out of Harvard,
thereby sabotaging my grandfather's hopes and dreams,
and he drank. He drank a lot.
Still, he knew how to entertain us kids.
More than once
he snatched a quarter.
from one of my ears.
Later, when I caught him palming an ace,
I never told my younger brother.
For him, Uncle Charlie could never lose face,
so we didn't tell him that his "hero"
who never wanted to be great
was blown to bits
in a cathouse near Saigon
while drawing to an inside straight.

Along the Lake

Lighted streetlamps at lakeside
provide circles of light
in which tree shadows dance
as the wind picks up
before the rain.
Unseen but heard,
the surf repeats and repeats
its pulsating refrain.
I remember my Father's words,
In a sharp wind, shallow lakes
kick up quickly.

Suicide in Blawnox

The soothing sound
of a train whistle at night
is once for me
a wistful call to travel
to far-off lands
until I learn
of a woman in Blawnox
aroused by the sound
who throws herself
in front of an oncoming train,
having failed days before
to kill herself
with an overdose of pills,
and I wonder
what overriding force,
what series of ills
could have caused her
to pursue such a course.
The whistle's call now conjures up
the image of this wailing woman,
suffering an unknown ailment
with nightgown billowing
running at full speed to experience
life's final derailment.

Beating the Rain

Dark night.
Pounding rain
Black mood.
Frozen thoughts.
A locomotive's
far off refrain
brings me to my senses
such as they are.

Squaw Valley Park

My customary bench
provides a vantage point
near the swing sets
in Squaw Valley Park.
In front of me
a Grace-Kelly lookalike,
a blond princess,
reveals her adoration
as she pushes a giggling infant
whose blond curls
match her mother's golden mane.

Further down, a man is pushing
a black-haired toddler.
The man armed with tattoos
is scruffy in black pants
and high black shoes.
He is no handsome prince,
and yet, his face
records the same smiling adoration.
despite what the blond princess
might describe as an obvious lack of breeding.
When they in unison spot me staring
I drop my eyes and pretend I'm reading.

Saturday Matinee

Magnificent theatres
on the weekends call to me and George,
a friend who later became a victim of cancer.
A short distance down Sheridan Avenue
they wait for us offering Roy, Tyrone, Errol and John.

Convinced back then
of our own invincibility,
and that of our heroes,
we refuse to believe
that we could ever die.
Soon enough
girls begin to seduce our deepest thoughts
and provide our latest fun,
dispelling our former heroes,
one by one.

Still, I wish we could return
to that world of make-believe
when time was suspended,
and intermission was never sought.
A world in which on-screen cancer could never kill,
even if cancer was part of the plot.

Rip-Off

It ripped
through Highland Park
like a meteor.
Mrs. Vogle on Wellesley Road
happened to see them—
two naked figures across the street
in a backyard pool, swimming,
young and married,
but not to each other,
a liaison not at all discrete.
It found Mrs. Vogle
and her cronies
lapping up the muddy news
like cattle at a trough.
This was the sixties
when the F-word was rarely used
and the experience of snuffing cocaine
was as foreign as Garbo.

Too soon Hollywood's evil
invaded even Mrs. Vogle's pristine street.
If she had known then
where it was all headed—
the overall degradation,
the persistent lack of meaning—
she would have ignored the naked figures,
closed the curtains,
and kept right on cleaning.

New Perspectives

Always curious,
I wonder at my parents' locked door,
on a Sunday,
a day when my father is at home.
A moan from within
prompts a question—*Mom,
are you all right?*
Giggles precede
my mother's stoic reply—
*I'm fine, dear.
Just fine.*

Along the creek at Fredericktown
I spot someone's hand-picked flower
lying closed on the muddy bank.
When my finger extends
to touch its rosy petals
I'm certainly not prepared
to see batwings opening
and a tiny snarling face
showing teeth razor-sharp and bared.

Poochie, a neighbor and I,
are on our way to the store
when a long, black car
stops beside us—
Your little brother looks so tired,
the face says.
Let me drive him down the hill.
I think, What a nice man.

Poochie, years older,
is of a different view.
The later enlightenment
that enshrines Poochie's act
leaves little to be said.
It seems clear to me
that without his intervention
I most certainly would be dead.

My Uncle is a Steering Knob

My uncle is a steering knob.
My memory wants to make him
big and barrel-chested.
Still, there's no face,
just the feeling of being on his lap
behind the steering wheel of his car.
There is something about that knob,
perhaps a nude or a pretty girl inside.
Even at five, I wanted to see.
DON'T TOUCH THAT!
And as he spoke these harsh words,
his face disintegrated.

My Sister was a Warner Brothers Wannabe

My sister, a Warner Brothers wannabe,
spent three years shacked up
with a producer
in New York City.
Some career—
no college,
eighteen years' old,
fucking for radio parts.
But, oh, what a voice!
Over Christmas,
in a voice that was sultry and serene,
she'd sing while washing the dishes,
Smoke Gets In Your Eyes,
Blue Moon and other favorite tunes
as I listened, quiet and unseen.
When Dad
brought her back home for good,
I was only twelve,
but I'm the one who knows for sure
how good she could have been.

Indian Display

Eight years' old
and separated from my parents
I encounter a display
at the museum
inside a glass case—
an Indian near-naked
with war paint in place
is lifting a bloody scalp
from an unfortunate victim
who is lying on his face.
Until age ten that same aborigine
comes for me
each time the rain pounds
and thunder roared
making me fearful,
but never bored.

I'm Here on my Deathbed

God, please listen.
I'm here
on my deathbed,
with curtains drawn
in a room that smells of death.
The doctors tell me
I've got a blood disease
I can't even pronounce.
They tell me I'll soon be dead.
I never thought
this would happen to me.
I thought I was a favorite,
a real contender,
so help me to solve
what has become
a real mind bender.
Have you and I fallen
into some mysterious estrangement?
Please respond quickly.
If you don't come through soon,
I may want to make
a different arrangement.

Butterfly

Her very first baby word was
Butterfly.
A short time before her death
my mother gives my father and me
that memory.

In a corner of his room
Dad sits alone,
frightened and depressed,
after learning
there can be no replacing her.

We children ask questions
regarding her affection:
Where did control
leave off
and love begin?

With no words spoken
she could bend
our will (and his).
Her eyes would reveal
new ways of pleasing her.

Such issues
are lost on Dad.
In the state of grief he is in,
he is unaware that very few butterflies
survive the pin.

Dunmoyle

Even on clear days it rained
(or so it seemed).
Everywhere the mud
was up to our knees.
The worst threat
came from German snipers
who infested the area like fleas.
Anyone whose mind wandered
for as much as a split second
would become easy prey for one of these.

A strange thing happened a month ago.
We were returning from an attack
(those of us who made it back)
when the enemy began shooting at our backs.
Dunmoyle was hit and fell onto our own wire.
He was hung up good,
but wasn't about to expire.
He began screaming at top voice,
completely out of his head.
We sat in our holes and listened
knowing that anyone who tried
to save Dunmoyle
would end up dead.

Three brave men on separate runs
got killed trying to save him.
We felt sure that by nightfall
he would have passed
and, sure enough, as light faded

we heard him breathe his last.
Then the whole company began
saluting Dunmoyle while we were still under cover
Good morning, Private Dunmoyle,
and How did you sleep, Private Dunmoyle?
He was hanging on the wire staring at us,
upright as if ready to run,
a mascot in the form of a corpse.
It was hilarious, a load of great fun.
Then Dunmoyle started to stink
and the game came undone.

Elmira

I've read about what the Gorilla said
at Gettysburg in '63.
If I'd been in attendance
I'd have shot the bastard dead.
Elmira was operating then,
a man-made hell,
an appalling disgrace.
My father,
who was a prisoner there,
died a week before the Gorilla
showed his face.
Father's burial in unhallowed ground
will be of little note
nor long remembered,
except by our family of eight.
Two of my six brothers died
at Chickamauga and two at Pea Ridge.
That leaves just two of us
to carry on our campaign of hate.

D'Aleppo

I was SS once.
I'm 82 now in failing health,
living in Argentina.
I'm being tried *in absentia*
despite my post-war achievements,
and my accumulated wealth,
for something that occurred long ago
at D'Aleppo.

Italy was in crisis then.
The Axis powers were losing the war.
When the partisans began chopping at our heels,
my men were anxious to even the score.
Then we came upon D'Aleppo,
a tranquil little village
whose men were all away,
leaving the women and children
as our easy prey.

I remember it was a pretty town
with roses prominent on every corner.
The unlucky remnant was hauled
into the killing area we chose
where machineguns did their worst.
The blood ran red as the reddest rose.

No one now remembers this event.
It was an unfortunate
but necessary act of war.
Don't you see?

When reprisals are imposed,
innocent people must die.
The victims of D'Aleppo
will remain dead whatever happens to me.

*Let me step in here.
I'm a priest who was present
on that fateful day.
Hiding in the bell tower,
I could observe
what took place
in the square below.
Pure evil was unleashed on that day.
Man's universal soul
was blemished so thoroughly
that the blot will never go away.*

*The men of D'Aleppo finally returned
bringing with them a grief
presaged to last a thousand years.
Their families lay slaughtered
in the town square,
confirming their worst fears.
Just because forgiveness
comes from the Lord
doesn't mean that pure evil
here on earth should always be ignored.*

*I'm aware of the person
I'm expected to be,
and I regularly teach others to forgive,
but as far as I'm concerned
the man under indictment today
has no further right to go free.*

*Instead, after a quick trial he should be
drawn and quartered
and hanged from the nearest tree.*

Blood-Red

Custer is dead.
On this hillside.
Barely conscious.
Nearly dead.
I lie spread-eagled,
eating mud
that is blood-red.
Indian squaws
are mopping up,
determined to torture
any trooper left alive.
I can observe what is intended for me
by simply turning my eyes.
Lord, let me die
before the savage death squad
arrives in force.

My perspective changes
after a final bleed
that spouts out of me, blood-red.
Floating like a ghost above my brutal bed,
I observe the squaws changing course.
However menacing their methods might be,
they see the futility involved
in torturing someone who is already dead.

Left Behind

While hiding in the officer's mess
a knot-hole gives me a view
of outside events.
The U.S. Army has arrived.
The SS guards have fled.
Cowardice in battle
is the charge that brought me here,
and is the reason I'm forced to stay.
The SS has left me on my own
to face whatever fate befalls me
on this disastrous day.
Surrender to the Americans.
is the only option.
Removal of my uniform
would risk execution as a spy.
If the murder squad of prisoners finds me first,
they will think up a hundred ways for me to die.
Like cornered animals, they never forget,
and my atrocities are well known.

I can see that the liberators are becoming unglued
at the sight of bodies piled high
and at the cries of the wretched survivors,
emaciated and wide-eyed,
who are clamoring for food.
I want to shout, *They're Jews.*
They're only Jews.
But the words don't come.
There's one soldier
guarding one of the exits to the building.

in which I'm hiding.
Thankfully, I speak enough English
to ask him for amnesty.
If he refuses, I'm as good as dead.
The name's Finkelstein, he says.
Nothing more need be said.

Becoming Part of Nature

We are Doughboys.
Recently arrived to support the line.
Standing in the rain.
Peterson beside me.
He is a handsome colleague
from a happier time.
In an instant.
Petersen lies dead in the mud,
his gear unpacked.
I'll never forget the sound.
SSSSSSSSSSSSSTTTTTT!
What good is a doctorate in Philosophy
or a Masters in French
if the dreaded sound that killed Peterson
finds me in the trench?

Ode to Benjy

Handsome you are, my Bengy,
in your coat of navy blue
but why risk a ground assault
when your forces are so few?

Admiral Porter had to have his way
as he searched for vicarious glory.
He planned an attack upon a Rebel position
that is the subject of this story.

Why should sailors attack on land
when their strengths are found at sea?
The beach around Fort Fisher
is no place for a swab to be.

How determined you look
as you charge across the sand
brandishing a cutlass,
and holding Porter's pennant in your hand.

Benjy is an officer of nineteen years.
whose men have learned to love him,
and he leads them now toward the fortress walls
with the Rebel horde above him.

Bengy twists before the palisade
his Navy coat turned red.
The sandy ground beside the walls
provides a pillow for his head.

Where's the glory, darling Bengy?

You won't know a spouse's kiss
and you'll never hold your children.
That's a pleasure you will miss.

So when Porter wants the glory
what suits best must be the key.
The only way to avoid disaster
is to keep your men at sea.

An Ancient Eye

See there.
Soldiers marching.
My father says this
as he points to
an ancient photograph
hanging on the wall
of an Inn near Gettysburg.
Dark uniforms.
Muddy streets.
Bayonets fixed.
They must know
that battle is just ahead.
Which of the marchers
forever frozen in mid step
will in another hour or day or week
be permanently disabled or dead?

Rally

Swastikas, runes, pounding drums.
Soldiers in formation,
a sea of steel helmets and black uniforms.
Our leader comes.
(*Oh, look, there he is, there he is!*).
We crane forward to see,
and spot our swaggering honoree
strutting in the distance
through a passageway
opened for him between the ranks.
The scene is stirring,
unlike anything I've ever seen before.
From this distance, though, he looks so small.
Surely, a minikin such as this
could never bring us into another war.

South China Sea

I remember the display,
a short walk upstairs,
hidden, solitary, out of the way.
What a great Smithsonian find!
Portraits of young airmen
uniformed,
mustachioed,
gallant,
all brandishing green scarves
and painted by the same unknown artist.
I'm young enough then to think
there is glory and chivalry a war
in which no one dies,
and, at first, I envy the glorious pursuit
that brought them to those far-off skies.
Then I notice
the same small plate
under each painting.
Killed in Action
South China Sea
Each young man in that room,
however handsome or brave
lost his life
in the same watery grave.

Musings of a Death Camp Commandant

Denuded bodies
rolling upward
toward my slit of glass
form a pyramid of death
beneath my wide-eyed stare
into Gas Chamber XVI.
And, oh, the rush,
THE RUSH,
even now,
to see those twisted fingers
clawing upward
for relief that cannot come.
Despite the horror, I act with impunity.
Our valiant army is here to stay,
a force to last a thousand years.
Ten million jack-boots
now march on Europe's vanquished streets
producing a ceaseless cacophony.

Lost Body Parts

As a Union army surgeon,
I've witnessed what happens when
bone,
muscle
and sinew
are separated from
patriotism,
heraldry
and glory.
How many arms?
How many legs have I seen
stacked high
outside the window
in a pillar of gore?
The body parts become
the only fitting tribute
to the God of War.

Lawrence, Kansas
(Sacked for the second time on August 21, 1863)

Ah...the eyes—
sinister
grey-blue
frozen.
With ratty blond hair
and sunken cheeks
Even so, Quantrill, our leader, isn't ugly,
and he certainly isn't old.
Despite his young age,
he instills in the men a rage to murder
that makes them merciless and bold.
Before the raid on Lawrence,
in a voice of deep baritone, he shouts,
Boys, I want you to kill everyone.
Let the women and children be,
but shoot the rest,
anyone capable of carrying a gun.
Except for a few of us,
any thought of forbearance
is wiped away.

Lawrence, Kansas
appears to be ripe for the taking
on this sweltering day.
Four-hundred-fifty guerillas
charge the slumbering town.
Remembering Quantrill's direction,
most become deaf to any pleas for mercy,
and blind to any upraised hands.

Unarmed menfolk are shot at will
in front of terrified wives
whose screams are loud and shrill
as they beg for their lives.

As a teenage guerilla
fresh from a Missouri farm,
I become queasy
after seeing so many people killed.
I want to fly, ride away,
but I know that desertion is not treated lightly
and so, after each murder raid, I elect to stay

Hijinks During the Grand Review

At the Grand Review
spectators are cheering.
as each Union Corps marches past,
when out of nowhere
comes a galloping Custer
on a "runaway horse"
following what for him
is an unchartered course.
Is it possible that instead of grand-standing,
he has lost control of that steed?
General Grant thinks not.
There's no way that such a thing could happen.
Think of the many charges at full gallop
that this man has led—
this hero of Gettysburg,
this boy general,
this unequalled equestrian force.
A flustered Custer
just isn't something to consider
and that same critical assessment
would also apply to his horse.

Goya's Revenge

Francisco, you move me
with your drawings of the war.
The style you choose intrigues me
like nothing I've seen before.
Murder and brutality are everywhere.
Seemingly, you hang a corpse from every tree.
To unleash such horror,
how black your moods must be!
Did your Duchess take her leave?
Has your deafness exacted its toll?
Francisco provides his answer:
It's no mere mood.
I paint what I see.
If horror is depicted,
it exists in the world
not inside of me.

Winston Envy

Brave in spirit
when the country needed courage,
articulate when the right words were due,
resolute against compromise,
and oh, he knew, he knew
what his destiny would be.
He called it following his star.

I'm always moved by his
portrait—
blood-red tunic+
helmet in hand—
ready to test the Boers,
or lead a charge at Omdurman.
Whereas he saved the *blessed plot*,
to date, quite frankly,
I haven't accomplished a lot.

Instead, I'm doddering
into my sunset years,
the same used by him
to exhibit determination and courage
while quashing the Nazi menace,
a comparison that for me has become
the worst kind of penance.

Body Double

Alexander
often vaulted enemy battlements alone
leading the charge
with vermillion cloak billowing,
armed in greatness.
like a living god.
I'm made of the same components—
skin and bone
brain and vein
a heart pumping blood
that is just as red.
It's reassuring to know
that overriding hubris
and world conquest
didn't change the facts.
His body took on the same foul odor
that mine will experience
when the time comes for me to be dead.

Upon Observing a Photograph of Hemingway in His Later Years

Your feelings are evident
in the vacuous eyes
that once were piercing and bright,
the furrowed brow
corrugated with concern.
I suspect that one question plagues you—
What will happen when I can no longer write?
You conclude that you must act quickly
before your brain has turned to slate.

The gun closet,
I must find the key
before it's too late.
Still in your pajamas
your hair in a tangle
you free the lock
remove your favorite shotgun
and place its barrels
in your mouth
at the perfect angle.
The earsplitting report
triggered by your toe
sends pieces of your brain
splattering.

Papa, oh, Papa,
if we could read your intentions
in those tortured eyes,
why couldn't they?

No, it's worse than that.
Mary left the key
in plain view.
Mindless heroes were never
her cup of tea,
luckily for you.

I'm James Dean

Listen and you'll hear them--voices from the past.
I'm Napoleon. I want to conquer the world.
I'm Hitler. I want to do what Napoleon couldn't do.
I'm James Dean. I want to go faster.
I'm John Belushi. I want to fly higher.
I'm Elvis Pressley. I want to be the King.
Instead, each becomes a cold corpse
after experiencing a fall.
Ah, but how different the beginning was:
fame, riches, power, success.
They had it all
until the Fates stepped in
to shift the load
Next, came Russia, Waterloo,
a bunker burning,
two overdoses,
and a body lying lifeless in the road.

Hubris

Maestro, when our human pyramid expanded
from three to seven on the high wire,
you used the occasion as an excuse
to take away the net.
Didn't you see that such a step
would be something you'd regret?
When the pyramid collapsed,
you were the only one
who wasn't destroyed or crippled
beneath the unforgiving wire.
As the participant at the highest level
wearing a blue-sequined costume,
I had the furthest to fall.
Later, you returned to your solo skywalks
rather than retire.
During your famous handstand
above a yawning gorge
they heard your favorite refrain—
God is directing me—
as if the Fates would permit you
to cheat the Grim Reaper once again.
On that day, they watched you fall.
Maestro, the gods never intended
for mortals to have wings.
Unlike hubris, which is available to all,
invincibility is reserved for Princes and Kings.

Homage to Shelley at Seaside

A sudden squall
sufficient to swamp his craft
causes death by drowning,
prompting Romantic artists and poets
to imagine their dead hero
face-up and handsome on the sand,
a washed-up Adonis,
depicted as retaining his looks
in their paintings and in their books,
except that this Adonis
had been floating for ten long days,
enough time to affect a startling change in his looks.
An accurate picture would have been ugly and messy
so the Romantics cleverly made other plans.
In place of a truthful depiction,
they chose to restore the flesh
on their dead poet's face and hands.

Being Etta Place

It's as if Sundance,
your handsome cowboy lover,
plucked you full-grown
from a cloud of mist
giving life to a spell-binding beauty
tall and thin
ready to be kissed
with perfect speech
and tender graces
dressed in stylish clothes
obtained from the East
and other such places.

A superb horsewoman
and a crack shot
with auburn hair
tousled loosely
or tied in a serious knot,
you cast a spell
that makes men delirious.
Had you materialized out of the sea
adorned in a bejeweled coronet
you would have been no less mysterious.

An important member of the Wild Bunch,
you curse Butch and Sundance
for posing for a photo
in a far-off place,
that gives the Pinks
a chance to update each wanted poster

with a brand-new face,
and when the lawmen's pursuit
becomes too hot,
you freely agree
to travel with Butch and Sundance
to a far-off spot.

When the law in South America gets too close
you return to the states alone
like a departing ghost,
unwilling to witness the death
of the two men you favor most.
Researchers have often
designated you a "mystery woman,"
an integral part of western lore,
but no one will ever know
whether you were a frustrated heiress,
a former school teacher
or a talented whore.

A Key Lesson

While in D.C. recently,
I visit the site of the Star-Spangled Banner
where the portrait of Francis Scott Key
is prominently displayed,
a handsome man depicted in all his glory.
His heroic deeds in Baltimore harbor
in 1812 are well known,
but I wonder—how many visitors
are aware of the rest of the story?
In 1859, a scandal breaks
that severely damages the Key family name.
Barton Key, the great man's son,
achieves a different kind of fame
when he is shot dead in broad daylight
in Lafayette Square.
Fortunately, by then, his famous father has died.
At first, it's difficult for the public to understand
why the murderer, a prominent Congressman,
would perform such a crime,
but soon, they learn that
Barton Key is spending much of his time
with Rep. Daniel Sickles' beautiful wife
whereupon Sickles sets out fully-armed
to take the adulterer's life.
The assailant's fury knows no bounds
as reflected by his election
to shoot Key at close range
with an excessive number of rounds.
Edwin M. Stanton, Sickles' lawyer,
argues that his client

is temporarily deranged,
the first time such a defense
is ever utilized in court.
Acquitted of the crime,
Sickles goes on to become a war hero
after his career is revived.
Although it may seem somewhat perverse,
the final irony is that the young adulterer
is murdered by a man
whose reputation as a womanizer
is ten times worse.

Blitzkrieg

Time is a Panzer,
the kind we see
in old newsreels,
grinding onward
even as it bucks upward
over trenches
and bunkers,
unstoppable, deadly.
All the while
terrified faces
trapped in front
are convinced
that nothing can stop
its pounding tread.

Ours Are Do-Nothing Days

Ours are do-nothing days,
as contrasted with those our predecessors stressed
as they ventured over deserted prairies
content with being jostled and jolted
so long as their wagons were heading west.
Recall Shackleton or Perry
or Teddy Roosevelt at San Juan Hill.
Think of Lindbergh or FDR or Buffalo Bill—
heroes all, of the type we no longer see.
Instead, we fret over tee times on the Sabbath
or the number of invitations extended for tea.
Our ancestors proved their strength
by recovering from the Crash
without Social Security and with very little cash.
In the early years, a pregnant woman
risked her life when the baby first showed its head.
If the pelvic area wasn't large enough,
either the baby or the mother faced the happy prospect
of ending up dead. And here's the rub—
our sole objective today is to make lots of money
so we can join the right golf or country club.
Our idea of excitement is
to break eighty on the course, or to cavort
at Club picnics and dinners with the right social set.
Our ancestors can only wonder:
How boring can it get?

Great Works Bring Everlasting Fame

Great works bring everlasting fame
that even time and the grave cannot defile.
However, some great works don't reach their potential
until after the author is dead,
which sometimes takes awhile.
I won't stand for that type of fame
even for a minute.
Instead, I'll shun centuries of post mortem celebrity
for one hour of fame in the world while I'm in it.

As Time Goes By

I'm at a piano bar
alone and out of town
writing poetry on a paper napkin.
The inveterate blonde
in a red evening gown
is singing at the keys—
you must remember this—
reminding me
with full-throated ease
that time goes by.

Time Doesn't Leave Us Alone

Time doesn't leave us alone.
Today's baby girl
becomes tomorrow's toothless crone,
and our beloved general
with a hero's crust
becomes in time
a solitary gravestone
over a pile of dust.

Watch Out

Even if you're content,
and happy with what you've got,
I still must say watch out,
and recently I've been saying it a lot.
For what it's worth,
the Freemasons have chosen 2022
as the final year of our existence on earth.
Their prophecy is embedded
inside a small pyramid
at the top of the Washington Monument,
which was built by members of their sect.
For obvious reasons,
it makes sense to determine
whether their prediction is false or true.
Is the Freemason prophecy
worthy of our trust?
After all, Doomsday
is only a few years in the future,
unless that prediction is a bust.

Yeah, I know,
people have been predicting
the world's demise for many years.
The Mayans were dead wrong about 2012,
although their prediction certainly
added to our fears.
On the other hand,
if the Freemason prophecy
turns out to be correct,
the Mayans were only off by ten years,

which isn't all that bad.
Some say the Freemason prophecy
shouldn't be believed,
even though they've always had
impressive members in their fold,
like George Washington
and others equally as bold.
If it turns out they hold the key,
we must wonder what the catastrophic event
is likely to be—a giant asteroid?
Nuclear war?
At this point,
we can only guess.
We'll never know for sure.

Where Did It All Go?

As a toe-headed boy,
I once stood on a wobbly chair
to study a fresh face
in the bathroom mirror,
a reflection that today is replaced by
a worn-out replacement,
corrugated by wrinkles and creases,
and crowned by a silver crop of hair
whose thinning process never ceases.
Where did it all go?
I'm aware generally that all living things
must eventually pass.
Still, the thought of being mortal
wasn't foremost in my mind
until I began to study closely
my decrepit visage
in the bathroom glass.
Where did it all go?
At my age
there is no time for greatness.
No urn for a warrior's dust.
No ringing epitaphs—
only decay and rust.

Aged Fruit

Whose hands are these,
crooked and worn,
fumbling with my shirt buttons,
showing skin like a rhino's hide?
Whose eyes are these
staring at me from my mirror
through wrinkled enclosures?

Aged and worn,
such features as these,
cannot be associated with me,
don't you see?
I'm forever my father's son,
a fledgling,
still reaching for the forbidden fruit
on the family apple tree.

Dust to Dust

The strongest and the brightest
often feel that they
are on a higher plane,
until death, the great equalizer,
turns all to dust.
Stable boys and kings
show the same amount of rust.

Footprint

Relentless in its pursuit
time blots out, erases, eliminates
the dirtiest marks
like rain in a muddy footprint.

The Bullet Train

Imperfect as we are, it's nonsense to assume
that we're given only one chance
to perfect our lives
before ascending into heaven.
The Bullet Train confirms my thinking.
The Ticket Agent
tells me that I must pick
my most memorable age and year.
I ask a flood of questions,
hoping to understand
what he is saying.
For example, if I select 1955,
will I experience only that year,
or the balance of my life
from that year onward?
The agent only smiles and shakes his head,
knowing that it's futile to expect understanding
from a person who is dead.

Time is Now No Friend to Me

Time is no friend to me,
often revealing
facial wrinkles, furrows and creases
that weren't there in any prior year.
I remember as a youth
trying to halt time's
relentless pounding
under the roaring waterfall
in the creek at Fredericktown
inside an air pocket
behind surging water
until my father pulls me out.
It doesn't work.
There is no delaying
this relentless pursuer,
no reprieve.
Time pounds on
despite our effort
to duck,
or bob
or weave.

Lucinda in Pursuit

Lucinda looking refined and fresh
with your black hair done up,
you look elegant in your gown of black satin.
You and I were once together for a summer
until I moved away. Back only recently,
I've not had a chance to call on you,
and trapped by a lackluster date
here at the Cinderella Ball
I dare not approach.
Lucinda, you must give me a sign.

Now I see you're adjusting your shoe.
I wonder if you know, Lucinda
that as you bend and reach,
I'm able to study your luscious breasts.
You give me a wink as you begin to stand?
Lordy, Lordy. Like Moses I've reached
the Promised Land.

The Big Bang

Your email stuns me—
It's over for me, you write.
I'm not willing to pursue this relationship any longer.
Take good care,
and this after eight months of intense feeling between us.
Flowers and phone messages bring no response.
Your reaction sends me reeling.
Once well-placed in the universe
I now feel like I'm standing
one step too close to a black hole
that will stretch me beyond feeling.

Swoosh

I imagine Lilith
being pushed
off the subway platform
into the path of an oncoming train,
a move that puts her, still alive,
between the wall of the platform
and the side of one of the cars.
It is what they call a *corkscrew effect*
that leaves her able to communicate
so long as the car remains in place.
When the car is removed, however,
there is a SWOOSH sound
as her body uncoils
in a way that flushes her entrails
onto the tracks.
This vivid image
comes to me
on the day
Lilith announces
that our relationship must end
because she's leaving me for Damion,
my very best friend.

Lucinda in Peril

Two policemen shout,
Get to higher ground.
The dam is about to burst.
With my parents,
I run up our hill
expecting the worst.
Minutes later a roaring sound
mixed with human cries.
precedes the appearance
of a watery avalanche.
When a giant whirlpool appears,
survivors on floating debris
discover an additional terror
as they twist slowly round and round
before being propelled
into a vortex
further down.

I spot Lucinda
twisting slowly
in the whirlpool's embrace.
Not Lucinda! I shout,
begging Father to help
by trapping the raft
and pulling her out,
anything to help my classmate survive,
without telling him that I love her
and would sacrifice my own life
to keep her safe.
I'll never forget her expression,

beautiful, serene
with black hair frazzled,
hands folded
head bowed.
But our rope falls short
even when the raging waters
bring her close enough
to see the color of her eyes.
In another second, she is gone,
swept away despite our futile tries.
I still hear that roaring sound
mixed with human cries
even in the stillness of the day,
and I see Lucinda twisting slowly
as she waits to be taken away
while I stand safe and protected
on a spot too far away.

Blind

No mental portrait remains.
Were you the beautiful bride,
the brilliant student,
the caring mother,
the willing volunteer,
the sexy wife or
were you a neurotic, half-crazed alcoholic
who often raged through the house at night
throwing tantrums and every pot and pan in sight,
a person who at such times offered censure
so severe as to leave deep scars?
Who you were I cannot say.
Time has taken the correct image away.

Foxfire

You are foxfire,
a rare luminescence
seen on boggy ground,
a will-of-the-wisp
that is present, then gone,
only to reappear further on.

I would like to marry you,
to hold you,
but you slip quickly
through my fingers
like cold water
on a hot day.

How can I love a dragonfly?
I never know
where next you will light.
I might just as well
duplicate a hummingbird's
cruising speed
or kiss a butterfly
in flight.

Harrier

A harrier she was
although she hid it well
behind silver-blond hair,
and clear blue eyes
that appeared to be generous and kind,
plus, she talked with an angel's voice
that brought Ariel to mind.
Because of her strategy
of hiding her real self at the outset
my love set in at an early stage.
An early warning system was sorely needed.
It could have ended
a plague of sleepless nights.
Even a Diamondback
gives warning
before it uncoils and strikes.

Gilberte

I'm out of the wind here on the veranda
reading *Plutarch's Lives*
when I notice a figure on the beach
strolling slowly in a long, white dress,
totally absorbed by her thoughts
and difficult to identify
because of the angle
of her wide brim hat.
I watch her and I wonder,
Have I seen this woman before?
Then I realize that this vision
reminds me of Gilberte,
my darling Gilberte.

Oh, Gilberte, how I once loved you.
How beautiful you were!
Black hair and green eyes.
What rose however full
could ever match
the glory of your red lips?
This woman sees me now.
She turns her head.
If only it could be Gilberte!
Too often now I see her
where she cannot be.

You see, the beautiful Guilbert
walked into the sea
and drowned herself
on that dreadful day

when I had to be away.
Married to me, she despaired of a younger man,
who jilted her.
On the day he was to take her away,
he left her alone at the train station.

They found her face-down
floating in the waves,
her white shawl snaking through the water
like a reptile's tail—
curling, curling, curling.
Oh, Gilberte,
how you broke my heart that day.

Until then I knew nothing of your affair with Marcel,
or of your plan to steal away,
although I did know by then
that you had stopped loving me:
You care more for your gold than you do for me,
you said. Oh, my dear,
if you had only known.
I'd have given up my gold and even a throne
(if I had one)
just to hear you say
that you loved me only.
The woman on the beach is passing now.
I wonder,
Should I ask her to join me for lunch?

Lucinda

Lucinda,
the beauty of the day
pales by comparison
to your own radiance.
Sweet Lucinda, no chorus of nightingales
however steadfast
could ever outdo the dulcet tones
that emerge from your magnificent lips.
I see you above me now,
dear wife,
your hair golden yellow
in the afternoon sun,
as you stand
on your balcony.
Here I am
in the courtyard below
writing this poem
as I sit on my favorite chaise
watching you.
gorgeous Lucinda,
my angel.
I wonder how can you love me
so intensely?
After all, you're
so much younger than I.
You should love
someone like
Gorgio, not me,
young and handsome as he is.
Although poor

(the starving sculptor)
Gorgio is very creative.
He is with you now
up there on your balcony
putting into place
the stone obelisk
that he has sculpted for
my sixtieth birthday.
Lucinda,
you are singing now
as you watch Gorgio put the obelisk
into place.
He strains. This object is heavy. His bulging muscles
don't seem to attract you.
But wait!
Both of you are behind the object now.
Why are you both pushing forward?
I wonder, should I move?
I'm directly in the object's path
should it topple. Perhaps I—

Time to Walk the Ocean Floor

A dive into windrippled waters.
A multi-colored descent.
Emerald to azure.
Azure to slate grey.
Slate grey to coal black.

Searchlights highlight sunken ships.
Rusting in tangled mass.
A troopship
with five thousand souls
bombed and strafed
so quickly
that none escape.
A freighter lost with all hands.
Fathers and sons.
Cooks and captains.

I search in vain for their remains.
All are gone.
There is no trace.
No bony fingers pointing.
No grinning skulls.
It is as if the sea is so mortified
by our murderous acts
that it strains to dispose of the evidence.

Dreams by Moonlight

Years ago, after kissing Leola at lakeside
under a radiant moon,
I was encouraged to think
that our love wouldn't end soon.
Marriage, children, a circular drive
were pleasant images that I could foresee.
Naïve and young as I was, however,
I was unaware of the moon's inconstancy.
Eventually, Leola couldn't hide
her preference for significant family money
that only a mogul could provide.
When a suitable candidate appeared,
I was quickly given the boot.
To win her back, I persevered
in my pursuit, and in time
became quite rich.
Still, even after a very poignant demand,
I couldn't talk Leola into leaving this guy,
which means I must change the strategy I'd planned,
and wait for the bastard to die.

Aquatic Creatures

Blue and red splashes of light
behind my closed eyelids
lead me naked and free
to a deep pool
within a darkened cave.
Even in the half-light I see
aquatic creatures
swirling, bending, turning in graceful glide
never colliding, always free
and, despite their blindness,
able to see.

A Coach and Four

A coach and four
clatters through an open gate
onto a cobblestoned courtyard
scattering chickens and dogs
before stopping
at the Inn's front door.
Craning heads
from courtyard windows
watch as one man in livery
approaches the coach door
while a second attends to
the steaming horses
black as night and big.
The onlookers watch
as a robust man emerges
with frock coat shining,
adorned in silk stockings
that match his pure-white wig.
Make way for the King,
the attendant in livery shouts
while holding one horse's bit.
And right away I know
I've tapped into the dream
of some unsuspecting Brit.

Dreams

Dreams—
do birds have them?
Do they dream at all?
Scientists tell us
that when geese fly south,
it's because of an implanted call—
automatic, irrepressible, spontaneous—
without any need it seems
for any sort of mental process
that might be associated with dreams.
If reflection through dreams
is restricted to humans,
how thankful we should be.
Dreams permit us to reach for the stars
and to blend our souls with the universe
while remaining entirely free.
So long as I keep dreaming
and quell the temptation
to think with my mouth,
I'll never be found in a flock of geese
automatically flying south.

Pinch-Penny

Years ago,
when I lived beside my friend Jennie,
she and I used a special name
for her grandfather.
We called him *Pinch-Penny*.
All in black, he looked like a mortician–
black hat,
black pants
black coat,
black vest,
black boots.
A banker from the big city,
he came to our small town
to nurture his roots.
Numerous foreclosures
soon made him infamous.
Jennie lived with him
until an iceberg sank his ship.
The memorial service
was conducted in his name.
Jennie and I weren't at all surprised
when nobody came.

Poolside with the President

Poolside
rake in hand,
he removes leaves,
that we replace
behind his back,
not as an act of ridicule,
but to make sure
he has something to do.
We're assigned
to protect this tarnished icon
who once was
the leader of the Free World.
Completely lost,
the great communicator
never utters a sound.
All words are waterlogged
and all rational thought
has been drowned.

Matadors at the Slaughterhouse

Papa, you often watch
the matadors at the slaughterhouse
practicing their trade
with *espadas* in hand.
For you, artificial gimmicks,
such as horns on wheels
will never suffice
as a training device.
Instead, you direct
aspirants to train in the sand and mud
where the rugged beasts
stand ready to offer
their last spot of blood.
Papa, you once went so far as to say
that the thrill of the kill
justifies these pursuits,
adding that the killing of various prey
has kept you from killing yourself.
How ironic that your suicide,
which came after years of killing,
was the bloodiest act of all.
I'm now sure that you blew your head away
so that no one could skin it
and hang it on a wall.

Water Hole

Wildebeest are milling
at a water hole
in the Serengeti of my memory.
In an instant, scent
of lion propels
the herd
to take flight.
Watch now,
lion on the run
as they search
the choking dust
for faltering hooves.
It matters not
which of the many beasts is caught.
For such as these
death is forever fungible.

Do Horses Think of Suicide?

During the Yukon Gold Rush,
Dead Horse Pass
is the place where packhorses are shot
before being pushed over the side
into a gorge many feet below.
The story goes that one brave mare
with valuable packs secured.
charges over the edge on her own
before any firearm can be used.
Could this have been an equine suicide?
I'm a priest who is present
to observe this act of final protest
by an animal that has been thoroughly abused.
Think on what confronts this brave mare
when she completes the steep climb to the top.
Up ahead is a man with rifle in hand,
Standing atop the bloody summit above the gorge
where many horses still screaming in final pain.
That this brave horse would choose to make a final stand
by selecting suicide as an alternative to human abuse,
is welcomed by a few of us as something quite grand.

Coo

The alley beside our house
is as wide as our basement stair.
From my bedroom window
I can study the eaves
and the pigeons nesting there.

Soon a compulsion
grips me,
overpowering and strange,
tied to a brand-new BB-gun
and the certainty of a shot
at point-blank range.

I open the window
with the care
an assassin might take,
and as I level the gun,
BB's roll to one end,
making a rattling sound
that a diamondback would make.

Why don't they fly away?
My hand is shaking.
My vision is blurred.
The last thing I want to do
is to kill this innocent bird.
But my finger on the trigger
isn't part of me.
It's inhabited by some external force
that isn't affected by conscience

or by any thought of changing course.

Ode to a Blue Jay

In the feeder out back
with chest outstretched
you bully your way into the seeds
forcing other birds
(mostly sparrows)
to forget their needs
and dart away in fear.

Your brethren are bullies, too
(even the "ladies,"
if that term even works).
All join you
to clear the decks
with a chosen course
that always begins
with a show of force.

The next day you are at it again
joined by your fellow thugs
who help you displace the smaller set.
Heaven knows,
I'd rejoice if a hawk
scooped you up into its nest
to devour you
in any way it thought best.

Suddenly I understood.
You had no choice in the matter.
If God made you and your brethren all bad,
He could easily have made

the rest of us all good.
Instead, we are left to plot
our own life's course
free from prodding produced
from any internal force.

Beyond the Beasts

Huge furry beasts,
making furtive sounds
travel each year
to their regular feeding grounds
confident that the salmon
will be spawning when they arrive.
Winter calls on them
to take to their dens,
and helps the salmon to hide.
Winter also shoos the geese
from their freezing ponds
in time for the annual ride.
Why can't the same GPS detector
that serves these animals so well
be installed in each human heart
to stifle our free-will urges
and keep us off the road to hell?

On Display

On a fencepost
outside my window
it sits,
majestic,
beautiful,
like some Egyptian sphinx,
cat-huge in its whiteness,
overseeing its domain.
A white flash
releases like a shot
revealing its goal—
a bird feeder some distance above,
inhabited by a single unfortunate dove.
Just as quickly
the day grows dark.
Could it be
that the universe
reacts when one determined feline
extends its claws and finds its mark?

Alice's Lament

When Alice returns to the looking-glass,
it's the spring of '38.
By that time her hair is short,
and she's gained
a great deal of weight.

The Cheshire cat's smiling countenance
is replaced by a penetrating glare.
My dear, he says,
I don't wish to be rude,
but you've taken on the shape of a pear.

Alice lets out a scream
that alerts the loquacious Queen of Hearts
who comes out of a nearby wood.
Alice watches the Cat disappear
and would gladly follow suit
by retreating the scene
if she only she could.

Publicity Blitz

Ideas and images
rush at me from all sides—
radio, TV, billboards, magazines—
a publicity blitz
expressed in a universal language of greed
that promises happiness following transformation,
if only I will spend money I don't have
to buy things I don't need.

Learning About Horses

We learn that a horse
will eat until its health is wrecked
if a bin of oats
is left unchecked,
much like the death camp survivors
who were offered
mounds of mashed potatoes,
mountains of roast beef,
rivers of gravy,
exotic soups, and
exquisite wines.
by well-meaning Allied troops
who killed their victims
with kindness.
As a member of the fat lobby,
I myself am a victim of
gluttony, so much so that horses speak out
in ways not always discreet:
*We aren't prepared to let you mount
until you begin to exercise moderation
when you eat.*
If they spot me, they laugh and grouse,
*Is there a Percheron or a Clydesdale
in the house?*

Will Zu Zu Come Through?

As her attorney,
I don't pull any punches.
Sexual defilement
is a very serious offense.
Are you willing to testify in Court
under oath that your father is guilty?
In the end, she is reluctant to bring him down.
After all, he runs the Bailey Savings and Loan
and just about every other business
in this backwater town.

Kong Wrong

You'd think that Ape
would've learned his lesson,
having met tragedy years before
atop that very same building
on the identical ledge.
Of course, a look-alike heroine is there
to despair when the Ape
falls over the edge.

But the mighty Ape
never has a clue.
At the theatre
when the flashbulbs pop
and the chains snap loose
that Ape makes an identical beeline
for the Empire State Building
and with heroine in hand
climbs to the very same roof.

The only new twist
comes with the latest Fay Wray.
This one causes
our emotions to splinter,
when we note that she's wearing
nothing more than a nightgown
on the top of a building
in the middle of winter.

Predictably, a squadron of planes
comes out of a cloud

offering identical airmen
with machine guns equally as loud.
Still the Ape foolishly thinks
that this time he won't be licked.
Falling downward,
at the twenty-second floor
he realizes
he might have been tricked.

Colossal Beans

As far as I know,
no one has ever written about
COLOSSAL BEANS.
Oh, we all know about Jack,
but his were only magic beans,
and everyone
has forgotten
that story anyway.

COLOSSAL BEANS
are never seen,
never touched.
never tasted.
Yet, we know
they're out there,
just beyond our reach,
waiting to make us great.

COLOSSAL BEANS
will cure our ills
and augment our skills,
if we can only reach one inch further,
dig one foot deeper,
sail one league further,
rise one mile higher—
to find them.

However far you go,
you'll never reach the beans,
so stop trying.

I should know.
I expired trying to find them.
When I passed over,
I got permission
to study the beans firsthand.
Let me assure you
that they are COLOSSAL
in a way you on earth will never understand.

Bugged

Imagine the stories
the grownup aphids relate
to the little ones
with popping eyes,
the tiny sap-suckers
who haven't yet grown
to full size.

Let them plant an egg in you.
Then, you'll find out.
You'll become the host, they shout.
The egg will hatch
and you'll be devoured
from the inside out,
so when you hear us yell
Wasp! Wasp! Wasp!
You've got to fly like hell.

One young blade has a question.

There's a hand up
in the back.

I want to tell you how I feel, he says.
You tell me that I'll become the host
for an attacking wasp
who will plant an egg inside me that will hatch
and make me its meal?

The grownups all nod.

*Who is it that makes these rules
and when can I appeal?*

Big Things Have Feelings Too

Because he's big and hairy
and ugly as sin to boot,
Big Thing will at first seem scary,
and not the least bit cute.

I suspect that his sudden appearance
will give you one heck of a fright
even if you're sleeping with your brother
and you're able to turn on the light.

I felt the same way
the first time I saw him
but in the end, he turned out to be very nice.
He'd show up every day to dance and play
and on Sundays he'd always come twice.

Mother and Dad couldn't see him,
so we played without their knowledge.
All went quite well with this arrangement
until it came time for college.

And don't be fooled by the assumption
that Big Thing doesn't ever cry.
When I left town for college
I thought he'd roll over and die.

In the end, though, I soon discovered
my departure was only part of the tale.
It was the fact I was going to Harvard
when he'd spent all of his college years at Yale..

A Pointless Exercise

As Ginger romps
a seagull squawks
causing a chase
across the sand.
In her exuberance,
Ginger fails to note
the difference between
a live bird in the air
and a shadow bird
on land.

Brain Suctioning Through a Tube

Setting—Narrative—Plot
You are the writer, dear brother.
I am not.
Just before the cancer destroys you
I pray for the chance
to suction your brainpower into my own head.
Unfortunately, prayed-for events
seldom come to pass.
Worms get to eat your talent,.
while I remain here pumping gas.

A Bad Rap

My voice is weak,
My legs are sticks.
My hair is thin and grey.
Yet they call me the God of War.
Believe me the title is no great honor.
I hold the position without prestige or pay.
Over years of experience I've come to see
that man will persist in his ugly pursuits—
world war, civil war, war of attrition,
border war, colonial war, holy war,
war of independence invasion, raid, strife,
ethnic cleansing, rebellion, partition, revolt,
uprising, massacre, hostility, conflict, struggle,
engagement, encounter, antagonism, holocaust,
resistance, confrontation, donnybrook,
showdown, insurrection—
all the while striving to reach a murderous perfection,
the war to end all wars, the final burst of fire,
and when that happens it's my earnest hope
that I'll be able to retire.

Three Troikas

Uncle Vanya senses my fear,
but remains convinced
the story is something I should hear.
He speaks in a rasping voice
while stroking his pure white beard.

With the bride and groom
in the last of three troikas,
the wedding guests depart,
proceeding toward Moscow
on a frozen, winter's night
that is destined to end in terror
from the very start.
The ever-present howling
is muted at first by harness bells shaken into action
by plunging hooves over snow-packed courses.
Soon the starving wolves
in three separate packs
are close enough to terrorize the faltering horses.
First one troika overturns, then another
spilling the occupants into the frozen snow.
The bride and groom
hold fast to each other
hoping to be the last to go.

Despite my terror and continuing dread
the story becomes for me,
a rite of passage tied to words,
a holy communion that I've been fed.

Aristototelian Musings

The cicada shell cracks open.
A seed becomes a tree.
A rivulet begins as a stunted trickle
then roars into the sea.
Our love is a glowing coal
impossible to hide
that bursts into flame
when our hot breath is applied.

Pricked

I've watched
as Fate pricked my bubbles—
BLIP, BLIP, BLIP, BLIP—
one at a time as success comes close.
The latest bubble of happiness
involves a possible marriage
with a widow over sixty-five.
I'd really like this to happen
so please don't...
BLIP!

Misplaced Humor

When my married daughter
first moved four hours away,
in jest I told my son-in-law
that I intended to make
regular weekend visits to Annapolis
if that would be okay.

When the color
drained from his features,
I realized that my feigned boldness
had been somewhat misplaced.
I discovered that humor inside families
must be done with delicacy and grace.

I'm concerned that my son-in-law
has never recovered
from my small dose of fake bravado
which might explain
his abrupt decision to move
from Annapolis to Colorado.

The Human Body is a Miracle

All systems function together:
skeletal, muscular, nervous, circulatory,
lymphatic, immune, digestive,
reproductive, endocrinal, and many others.
The study of cells and tissues alone
can be a life's work. There are multiple
muscles interconnected in miraculous ways
to prevent a rattling collapse of bone.
The skeletal structure is designed
to keep the human body upright
for an average of four score years and ten.
The heart's cyclic routine occurs 70
times a minute and then begins again.
What manmade device
could function so efficiently for so long?
And what analysis explains
the placement in our bodies
of the intricate network of arteries and veins?
There so much to take in
that doctors specialize in certain key parts
such as heart, eye, brain, hand and knee,
and study various diseases with symptoms
only they can see. To doubters
who wonder how such a perfect specimen
could have come to be, I say study the universe
before concluding that we came from apes
or something worse?

Acknowledgements

Kendra Adkins, the manager of Four Seasons Book Store in Shepherdstown, West Virginia, provided encouragement for all my writing endeavors including this book of poetry. My wife Shannon stood behind my writing endeavors, always ready with loving reassurances.

About the Author

Rick Taylor is a graduate of Pitt Law School and Denison University who presently resides in Shepherdstown, West Virginia. His poetry has been featured in *Eureka* and in *the California Quarterly*. "A Time to Walk the Ocean Floor" and "As Large as the Universe" appeared in Volume 25, Number 2 (2006) of Westview, a publication of Southwestern Oklahoma State University. In November of 2005 "Foxfire" was awarded third place in the 2005 Pennwriters Poetry Contest. On January 2, 2010, his poem entitled "Never Alone in the Cemetery" appeared in the *Pittsburgh Post-Gazette*. Several of his poems were published in *Good News*, a local newspaper. He is presently working on a compendium of short stories which he intends to publish in the near future.

www.ingramcontent.com/pod-product-compliance
Lightning Source LLC
Chambersburg PA
CBHW071520080526
44588CB00011B/1509